To..

With love from.................................

Date ....

The author asserts the moral right
to be identified as the author of this work.

Published by
Lion Publishing plc
Sandy Lane West, Oxford, England
ISBN 0 7459 2348 8
Lion Publishing
1705 Hubbard Avenue, Batavia, Illinois
60510, USA
ISBN 0 7459 2348 8
Albatross Books Pty Ltd
PO Box 320, Sutherland, NSW 2232,
Australia
ISBN 0 7324 0645 5

First edition 1993

Acknowledgments
Studio photography by
John Williams Studios, Thame

Where possible, the space allowed for
photographs is the standard print size
(6 x 4 in.); otherwise photographs will need
to be trimmed to fit the spaces allowed.

A catalogue record of this book is available
from the British Library

Library of Congress CIP data applied for

Printed and bound in Singapore

A LION BOOK

OUR NEW GRANDCHILD

A Keepsake Album

Jean Watson

Introduction

Grandparents, like doctors, seem to be getting younger and younger these days! Seldom now do we find Grandma and Grandpa to be feeble and white-haired, ensconced in huge armchairs and nodding off beside a blazing log fire. Instead, today's grandparents are often free, fit and young enough to travel, sign up for courses and pursue interests and hobbies.

But whatever else has changed, the importance of the grandparent-grandchild bond is certainly not in doubt. If anything, given the current rate of family breakdown, this unique bond is needed more than ever. It is forged and maintained as grandparents spend quality time with their grandchildren. They can come to know and accept them; do things with them; slow down long enough to stand and stare with them at the wonder of living and growing things. They can pass on, perhaps by attitudes more than words, the ability to see life steadily and as a whole. They can help grandchildren see how special they are and how valuable their contribution is to the vast complex pattern of life in God's world. They can, in a word, love them, creating the best climate for their growth into whole, loving adults.

This book can be part of all that. Completing it will require thought, time and effort, making the finished work a deeply affirming personal gift from grandparents to a much loved and valued grandchild.

It would be wonderful if all children could grow up knowing each of their grandparents. But expected and unexpected events can prevent this happening. Even so, I address this book to both grandparents in the hope that those on their own will be able to fill it in not only for themselves but also on behalf of their absent partner. For it seems to me that though death or other forms of separation may physically part two people, one of them can—in the light of all their years of shared activities, thoughts and emotions—in a very real sense, continue to speak for the other.

Jean Watson

We welcome you

Jesus called the children to him and said, 'Let the little children come to me, and do not hinder them, for the kingdom of God belongs to such as these.'

FROM LUKE'S GOSPEL, CHAPTER 18

OUR FIRST PHOTOGRAPH OF YOU

YOUR NAME . . . .

NAME CHOSEN BECAUSE . . . .

. . . .

. . . .

YOUR DATE AND TIME OF BIRTH ..*August 27, 1997*
    4:14 A.M.

YOUR BIRTH PLACE ..*South Miami Hospital*
    Miami, Florida

YOUR WEIGHT ..*7 LBS. 10 OZS.*

YOUR HEIGHT ..*19 1/2 INCHES*

YOUR CHARACTERISTICS ..*Dark Hair.. Very Alert*
    and wanting to suck your
    hand, just like your mommie
    did, many years ago.

Y̲ou are welcome. As you are. Different from everyone else. We love you as you are now and as you will be at every age and stage. When you grow up, you will not have to win prizes or be more attractive or better at study or sport or making things than anyone else—you don't need to *prove* anything to us—before we will love you. Because our love for you is your gift for life. Love. Unearned and no strings. Love that is an unshakeable commitment to being your true friend, no matter what, for as long as we live.

L̲ove is the magic key of life.

EILEEN GUDER

*T̲he Lord bless you
and keep you;
the Lord make his face shine
upon you
and be gracious to you;
the Lord turn his face
towards you
and give you peace.*

FROM THE BOOK OF NUMBERS,

CHAPTER 6

The day you were born

YOU AND YOUR PARENTS

HOW WE FIRST HEARD THE NEWS WE WERE THERE! RANDY + JACQUES CAME AND TOLD US YOU HAD ARRIVED AND ALL THE FIRE ALA

THE WEATHER THAT DAY SOUNDED THAT WARM AN HUMID MORNING. IT WAS QUITE A WELCOME INTO THIS WORLD.

WHEN AND WHERE WE FIRST SAW YOU WE CAME IN TO SEE YOU WARMING, FUSSING AND TRYIN TO SUCK YOUR FIST.

HOW WE FELT WE WERE VERY THRILLED AND EXCITED YOO WERE HERE AND WE LOVED YOU EVEN MORE EACH PASSING MINUTE.

NEWS CLIPPINGS FROM THAT DAY

COPY OF YOUR BIRTH ANNOUNCEMENT

Anything that God makes is worth looking at. We live in no chance world. It has all been thought out. Everywhere work has been spent on it lavishly—thought and work—loving thought and exquisite work. All its parts together, and every part separately, are stamped with skill, beauty and purpose.

HENRY DRUMMOND

I see this baby leading me back to my beginnings, reopening rooms I'd locked and forgotten, stirring the dust in my mind by re-asking the big questions.

LAURIE LEE

Three generations

When we look at you we often think about your parent—our child—as a baby.

YOUR PARENT'S FULL NAME AT BIRTH . . . .

PLACE AND DATE OF BIRTH . . . .

MEMORIES WE TREASURE FROM THOSE YEARS . . . .

. . . .

. . . .

OUR CHILD, YOUR PARENT, AS A BABY

YOU AS A BABY, OUR GRANDCHILD

The faith of a baby . . . is particularly fused with sensual experience. Through bodily contact with the mother, the child receives the message that she is loved and wanted. Thus at this very early stage the foundation for our images of God and way of relating to God is laid.

STEVE SHAW

We are delighted that you are our grandchild and we're going to try to be the best grandparents in the world. Not spoiling you, but giving you treats and surprises. Not forever grumbling, but noticing what is positive and making our memories into stories for you to enjoy. Not disapproving of all the activities you like, but valuing your feelings and opinions as uniquely yours. Of course, all we can really be for you is ourselves. But it'll be the best we can be for you.

What we wish for you

May you find work that stimulates, fulfils, is worthwhile.

May you find meaning, challenge and enjoyment in life.

May you discover your true identity, reach your full potential.

May you excel in the one all-important R, the R of relationships.

May you grow strong and healthy in mind, body and spirit.

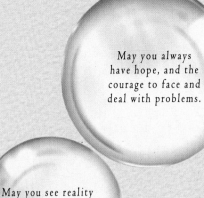

May you always have hope, and the courage to face and deal with problems.

May you find support and help in the dark and difficult times.

May you see reality and truth, even when it's painful.

May you give and receive love in a whole network of relationships.

May you accept and forgive—both yourself and others.

The kind of love with which God loves us... is one personal and sensitive enough to meet us as individuals, and big enough to stimulate and contain growth beyond our wildest imaginings.

RUTH ETCHELLS

MAKE A BUBBLE PICTURE

◆ Find a shallow container, like a lid or an empty carton, and partly fill it with some bright, non-toxic, liquid paint.

◆ Add a generous squeeze of washing up liquid.

◆ Insert a long straw (so the mixture won't splash up into your face) and blow into the mixture until the bubbles reach the rim of the container.

◆ Lay a sheet of paper over the top, then lift it off gently and quickly and you will have a beautiful bubble-pattern picture.

◆ You can lay the same paper over containers with other paints in them if you want a different effect.

Bless this child

Jesus took the children in his arms, put his hands on them and blessed them.

FROM MARK'S GOSPEL, CHAPTER 10

A PHOTOGRAPH OF YOU ON THE DAY
YOU WERE CHRISTENED/DEDICATED

PLACE, DATE AND TIME . . . .

. . . .

IT WAS YOUR SPECIAL SERVICE. A FEW OF YOUR SPECIAL FRIENDS PROMISED TO HELP
YOU UNDERSTAND WHAT LIVING AS GOD'S CHILD IN GOD'S WORLD MEANS.

THEIR NAMES ARE . . . .

. . . .

AFTER THE SERVICE THERE WAS A PARTY. SOME OF THE GUESTS WERE . . . .

. . . .

OUR GIFT TO YOU WAS . . . .

. . . .

SOME OF THE OTHER GIFTS WERE . . . .

. . . .

To be and to feel good in being oneself is the key to self-love, and self-love is the key to all personal loving, for unless we recognize our resources and feel these are good, we have nothing to donate to others, nor have we the means of receiving the love of others because there is no part of ourselves that is recognized as or feels good enough to be appreciated.

JACK DOMINIAN

A PRAYER FOR YOU

O God, let this child know and feel that she is loved by you, by her family and by her friends, so that she will be secure and happy enough to give her love to others. May she regard her assets of mind and body as gifts to be enjoyed and shared. May her life add to the world's healing rather than to its pain. May she be a builder of bridges rather than of walls. A mender rather than a destroyer. May she learn to make the most of her life—of herself and of all her relationships and experiences. May she distinguish what is bad, second-rate and trivial from what is good, excellent and worthwhile and make the best choices. Amen.

Family tree

Great Grandmother_____

        Grandmother_____

Great Grandfather_____

                  Mother_____

Great Grandmother_____

        Grandfather_____

Great Grandfather_____

                  Your name_____

Great Grandmother_____

        Grandmother_____

Great Grandfather_____

                  Father_____

Great Grandmother_____

        Grandfather_____

Great Grandfather_____

You're in a far-reaching family. Not just with those people you see every day, but with aunts and uncles and cousins. Here's a photo of some of your wider family.

I kneel before the Father, from whom the whole family in heaven and on earth derives its name.

FROM THE BOOK OF
EPHESIANS, CHAPTER 3

OCCASION . . . .

. . . .

PEOPLE IN THE PHOTO . . . .

. . . .

WHERE THEY LIVED THEN . . . .

WHERE THEY ARE NOW . . . .

. . . .

. . . .

Father of all, accept our thanks for the joys of family life. Help us to build with you the kind of family which welcomes the stranger, the lonely and the needy. Teach us through this small family to love the family of mankind and to realize our part in it.
Amen.

FRANK COLQUHOUN

My home is clean enough to be healthy and dirty enough to be happy.

PLAQUE FOUND IN A SCOTTISH
GIFT SHOP

Where we live

God . . . is at once the God of the above and beyond, the here and now, the then and there. Because he intervened in history at a particular place among a particular people, he has indicated for all time his concern with this moment, that location. And therefore my hour and my home and my place become God's concern.

RUTH ETCHELLS

WHERE WE LIVE

Home—the place where we grumble the most and are treated the best.

CHARLES M. CROWE

WHERE YOU LIVE

Everyone needs a place somewhere on earth. A place where they feel welcome and safe and at home. And it takes more than bricks and mortar to create such a place. It takes people: people whose love gives us the security, significance and space that we need.

As well as having our own private places, we all share one big place—the earth. And planet earth is not so much inherited from our parents and grandparents as borrowed from our children and grandchildren. It needs responsible, caring people to manage and look after it so that it goes on being a good environment and home for human beings.

Jesus said, 'If anyone loves me, he will obey my teaching. My Father will love him, and we will come to him and make our home with him.'

FROM JOHN'S GOSPEL, CHAPTER 14

PHOTOGRAPH OF THE AREA OF THE
COUNTRY IN WHICH YOU WERE BROUGHT UP

Christmas

Christmas is always special when there are children around. Our Christmas was extra special because the child who was around was our new grandchild!

YOUR FIRST CHRISTMAS

MEMORIES OF SOME OF THE CHRISTMAS CELEBRATIONS WE HAD WHEN WE WERE

CHILDREN. . . . .

. . . .

. . . .

CAROLS WE ENJOYED SINGING. . . . .

. . . .

. . . .

. . . .

Loving Father, help us remember the birth of Jesus, that we may share in the song of the angels, the gladness of the shepherds, and the wisdom of the wise men. Close the door of hate and open the door of love all over the world. Let kindness come with every gift and good desires with every greeting. Deliver us from evil by the blessing which Christ brings, and teach us to be merry with clean hearts. May the Christmas morning make us happy to be thy children, and the Christmas evening bring us to our beds with grateful thoughts, forgiving and forgiven, for Jesus' sake. Amen.

ROBERT LOUIS STEVENSON

One year old

You've been with us for a whole year. How you've grown! And what a lot you've learned to do. It's been fun watching you grow, just as we watched our child, your parent, grow from a newborn baby into an energetic one-year-old.

NOW YOU ARE ONE

YOUR PARENT AROUND ONE YEAR OLD

WEIGHT GAIN IN ONE YEAR . . . .

. . . .

HEIGHT GAIN . . . .

. . . .

HOW YOUR LOOKS HAVE CHANGED . . . .

. . . .

THINGS YOU CAN NOW DO . . . .

. . . .

. . . .

YOUR FIRST BIRTHDAY PARTY . . . .

GUESTS ON YOUR FIRST BIRTHDAY . . . .

. . . .

. . . .

PRESENTS YOU RECEIVED . . . .

. . . .

GAMES WE PLAYED . . . .

. . . .

*H*elp me to extract all possible fun out of life. There are so many funny things around us and I do not want to miss any of them.

FROM A NUN'S PRAYER

On the move

In the next year or so, you were on the move—and so were all sorts of objects, with your help! Of course, we moved dangerous items like bleach and knives before you got to them, but we still found some of our belongings in the funniest places:

....

....

Your hands became very busy too. Here's a photo of you and your busy hands:

And here's a recipe for modelling dough for small hands to busy themselves with!

MODELLING DOUGH

In a saucepan, heat the following:

- ◆ A cup of water. (Vegetable food-dye can be added to brighten the dough.)
- ◆ A cup of flour
- ◆ Half a cup of salt
- ◆ 1 tablespoon of cooking oil
- ◆ 2 teaspoons of cream of tartar

When the mixture begins to bubble, stir with a wooden spoon until it becomes stiff and forms a ball. Turn off the heat, let the dough cool... and play!

You also began to paint us pictures and make us things which were special because they came from you. We especially liked:

. . . .

We pray that your hands—and the rest of you—will keep busy doing things that make both you and other people happy: mending and making; helping and welcoming; playing and working. Amen.

Fun and Play

Mirth is God's medicine. Everybody ought to bathe in it.

HENRY WARD BEECHER

A PHOTOGRAPH OF YOU HAVING FUN

A PHOTOGRAPH OF US HAVING FUN TOGETHER

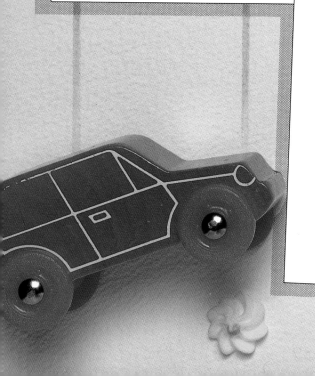

When we were children we had all kinds of fun activities: dressing up, acting goodies and baddies, playing with dolls and trucks and toy animals, tree-climbing and pond-gazing, going to the fair, listening to stories.

SOME OF THE TOYS AND GAMES WE ENJOYED ALL THOSE YEARS AGO:

....

....

I tell you the truth, anyone who will not receive the kingdom of God like a little child will never enter it.

FROM MARK'S GOSPEL,
CHAPTER 10

TOYS AND GAMES ARE DIFFERENT TODAY.
YOUR MOST LOVED TOYS AND GAMES:

....

....

FIRSTS

FIRST OUTING WITH US, YOUR GRANDPARENTS. . . . .

FIRST WALKED. . . . .

FIRST SOUNDS . . . .

FIRST WORDS . . . .

FIRST SMILE. . . . .

FIRST TUMBLE. . . . .

FIRST HELD UP YOUR HEAD . . . .

FIRST HOLIDAY . . . .

FIRST SAT UP ALONE . . . .

FIRST TOY . . . .

FIRST CRAWLED . . . .

FIRST FRIEND . . . .

FIRST TOOTH. . . . .

FIRST MORNING AT PLAYSCHOOL . . . .

FIRST STOOD . . . .

FIRST PAINTING. . . . .

The things you said

What children say can be amusing. It can also tell us quite a bit about who and where they are. About what they have or have not grasped clearly. About where we are or are not communicating clearly with them through language about the world in which they have begun to live and learn.

The baby's nose is falling down.

I never knew my granny when she was new, only when she was old.

I love you two hundred much.

Mum, where's heaven? Oh, I'll ask grandma. She's better at directions.

Is the dark on?

Who did the snow?

This is my breakdown truck. It goes along the road and breaks down cars.

Among the words a person uses, his body language, his feeling and thinking, we need also to listen to his silences which can mean many things . . . Listening to someone, then, is a multi-dimensional activity, complex, demanding and mutually enriching, for it is as we listen like this that we hear not only what someone is saying but also who he is.

ANNE LONG

He talks with a stagger.

The kettle's crying.

SOME OF THE THINGS YOU SAID . . . .

. . . .

. . . .

. . . .

School-days

Train a child in the way he should go, and when he is old he will not turn from it.

FROM THE BOOK OF PROVERBS, CHAPTER 22

A PHOTO OF YOU AT SCHOOL

YOUR SCHOOL-DAYS

THE TIME YOU LEFT HOME, AND HOW YOU GOT TO SCHOOL . . . .

. . . .

THE SUBJECTS YOU STUDIED . . . .

. . . .

FACILITIES AT YOUR SCHOOL . . . .

. . . .

WHAT YOU DID DURING BREAK-TIME . . . .

. . . .

YOUR SPORTING ACTIVITIES . . . .

. . . .

WE WERE AT SCHOOL FROM 19   TO 19   (GRANDMA)

AND 19   TO 19   (GRANDPA)

THERE WERE SOME SIMILARITIES BETWEEN OUR SCHOOLING AND YOURS . . . .

. . . .

. . . .

THERE WERE ALSO SOME DIFFERENCES! . . . .

. . . .

. . . .

I grow old learning something new every day.

SOLON

The entire object of true education is to make people not merely do the right things, but enjoy them; not merely industrious but to love industry; not merely learned but to love knowledge; not merely pure but to love purity; not merely just but to hunger and thirst after justice.

JOHN RUSKIN

God is always asking us to look more deeply at the truth, to avoid reaching superficial conclusions.

JACK DOMINIAN

By the seventh day God had finished the work he had been doing; so on the seventh day he rested from all his work.

FROM THE BOOK OF GENESIS,
CHAPTER 2

Trips and holidays

YOU'VE BEEN ON HOLIDAYS AND OUTINGS TO . . . .

. . . .

. . . .

A PHOTOGRAPH OF YOU ON A FAMILY OUTING OR HOLIDAY

SOME OF THE THINGS YOU COLLECTED. . . . .

. . . .

. . . .

OUTINGS WE REMEMBER GOING ON AS CHILDREN . . . .

. . . .

. . . .

A PHOTOGRAPH OF US ON HOLIDAY

THE PLACE AND PEOPLE IN THE PHOTOGRAPH . . . .

. . . .

Light and shadow

Life, like nature, is rich with changing patterns. And the different ages and stages of life are part of the pattern of human experience and development.

Grandchildren are in the early spring, while parents may be in the summer and grandparents moving towards the autumn of their lives. But friendship leaps across all age and stage barriers, even using them to enrich the relationship. And each stage has its light and shadow.

There is a time for everything,
and a season for every activity under heaven:
a time to be born and a time to die,
a time to plant and a time to uproot...
a time to weep and a time to laugh...
a time to keep and a time to throw away...
a time to be silent and a time to speak...

FROM THE BOOK OF ECCLESIASTES, CHAPTER 3

SOME OF THE TIMES IN YOUR CHILDHOOD WHEN
YOU HAD TO WORK HARD TO FIND A WAY FORWARD

. . . .

. . . .

SOME OF OUR OWN EXPERIENCES OF STRUGGLE . . . .

. . . .

. . . .

. . . .

I walked a mile with Pleasure.
She chatted all the way,
But left me none the wiser
For all she had to say.

I walked a mile with Sorrow,
And ne'er a word said she;
But oh, the things I learned
from her
When Sorrow walked with me!

ROBERT HAMILTON

Suffering can work inside us
in two possible ways. It can
drive us into a retreat of self-
pity, hardening our attitude to
others and diminishing our
interest in and enjoyment of
life. Or it can have the opposite
effect, so that we can grow closer
to God and perhaps become
more sensitive and
understanding towards other
people.

ANGELA ASHWIN

Shared memories

Over the years we have done a great deal together. Many changes have happened during this time so the memories we have of you are very precious:

SPECIAL EXPEDITIONS WE SHARED . . . .

. . . .

SPECIAL DISCOVERIES WE MADE . . . .

. . . .

JOKES WE'VE ENJOYED . . . .

. . . .

. . . .

. . . .

SPECIAL ANECDOTES ABOUT OUR FAMILY . . . .

. . . .

. . . .

. . . .

BOOKS AND STORIES WE LIKED . . . .

. . . .

GAMES WE PLAYED . . . .

LIKES AND DISLIKES WE SHARED . . . .

. . . .

SPECIAL FAMILY RITUALS AND OCCASIONS . . . .

. . . .

It is only with the heart that one can see rightly; what is essential is invisible to the eye.

ANTOINE DE SAINT-EXUPERY

We were struck by the way you saw things sometimes.

FOR EXAMPLE: . . . .

. . . .

. . . .

. . . .

. . . .

. . . .

. . . .

. . . .

Children are not cluttered up with as many unnecessary concerns as adults. They know how to stop and look and be totally lost in something exciting like a ladybird or a model engine. They are natural contemplatives. Finding again the simplicity of a child is not reverting to childishness; it is rediscovering a certain way of looking and trusting and receiving.

ANGELA ASHWIN

Learning to love

Infantile love follows the principle: 'I love because I am loved.' Mature love follows the principle: 'I am loved because I love.' Immature love says: 'I love you because I need you.' Mature love says: 'I need you because I love you.'

ERICH FROMM

We value our growing relationship with you. Through all our relationships we are learning to love and, with God's help, growing better at loving.

Love can be expressed in words. Here's what one eight-year-old boy wrote about his grandmother:

A grandmother is a lady who has no children of her own, so she likes other people's boys and girls. Grandmas don't have anything to do except be there. If they take us for walks they slow down past pretty leaves and caterpillars. They never say, 'Hurry up'. They are usually fat but not too fat to tie shoes. They wear glasses and sometimes they can take their teeth out.

They can answer questions like why dogs hate cats and why God isn't married. They don't talk 'visitors talk' like visitors do which is hard to understand. When they read to us they don't skip words or mind if it is the same story again. Everybody should try to have a grandma, especially if you don't have television, because grandmas are the only grown-ups who always have time.

A CHILD'S ESSAY QUOTED BY BETTY CARLSON

Now's your chance to write about us, your granny or grandpa—or both. You could add a drawing, perhaps!

....

....

....

Love is patient and kind; it is not jealous or conceited or proud; love is not ill-mannered or selfish or irritable; love does not keep a record of wrongs; love is not happy with evil, but is happy with the truth. Love never gives up; and its faith, hope, and patience never fail.

FROM THE FIRST LETTER TO
THE CORINTHIANS, CHAPTER 13

Making and keeping friends is a way of learning to love. Here are the names of some of your friends over the years:

....

....

The glory of the star, the glory of the sun—we must not be so full of the hope of heaven that we cannot do our work on the earth; we must not be so lost in the work of earth that we shall not be inspired by the hope of heaven.

PHILIP BROOK

PHOTO OF YOU LEAVING SCHOOL

Looking forward

When you were little, there were lots of things you wanted to be when you were grown up. Some were more practical than others! We remember you wanted to be:

....

Things have changed since then! When you finished school, you were good at:

....

....

....

....

....

....

SOME OF THE OCCUPATIONS CHOSEN BY YOUR FAMILY OVER THE GENERATIONS

. . . .

. . . .

. . . .

. . . .

. . . .

SOME OF THE ACTIVITIES WE WERE ABLE TO DO FOR THE FIRST TIME

WHEN WE LEFT HOME . . . .

. . . .

SOME OF THE THINGS YOU CAN LOOK FORWARD TO NOW . . . .

. . . .

. . . .

Am I one person today and tomorrow another?
Who am I? They mock me, these lonely questions of mine.
Whoever I am, thou knowest, O God, I am thine!

DIETRICH BONHOEFFER

At moments when the future is completely obscured, I thought, can any one of us afford to go to meet our tomorrows with dragging feet? God had been in the past. Then he would be in the future too. And with his presence had always come an end to tasteless living. Always he had brought high adventure—high hopes, unexpected friends, new ventures that broke old patterns. Then out in my future must lie more goodness, more mercy, more adventures, more friends.

CATHERINE MARSHALL

What I kept, I lost.
What I spent, I had.
What I gave, I have.

OLD PERSIAN PROVERB

It needs courage to let our children go,
but we are trustees and stewards and
have to hand them back to life—
to God.

ALFRED TORRIE

A new beginning

We have watched you grow:

HEIGHT/WEIGHT AT BIRTH . . . .

HEIGHT/WEIGHT FIVE YEARS LATER. . . . .

HEIGHT NOW . . . .

You will go on growing, not just taller and bigger but in every way, until you are ready to be independent: to leave home, make your own decisions, manage your own life. And loving you means, at the right time, letting you go, setting you free to do these things—to become your unique self.

As you try out your new freedom, rather like a fledgling learning to fly, we'll be caring, watching and praying as much as ever. And we look forward to a different, new, adult relationship with you.

Our prayer and wish is that our grandchild will enjoy the present, building up a past full of happy memories and looking forward with hope and confidence to the future. Amen.

PHOTOGRAPH OF YOU NOW

May the road rise with you,
May the wind be at your back,
And may the Lord always hold you
In the hollow of his hand.

A CELTIC BLESSING